Small Works

Pam Rehm **Small Works** Flood Editions, Chicago, 2005

For permission, required to reprint or broadcast more than several lines, write to:
Flood Editions, P.O. Box 3865, Chicago, IL 60654-0865, www.floodeditions.com
Poems included in this volume have appeared in *Five Fingers Review*, *Harrisburg
Review*, and at www.culturalsociety.org. The author wishes to thank the Cultural
Society for publishing some of these poems in a chapbook entitled *Saving Bonds*
(2002), and to thank Jeff Clark for designing this book. FIRST EDITION

Contents

When Poverty Is Unattainable 1

Forget Me Not 5

A Charm for Sleep 6

Summer 10

How to Stay Alive in the Woods 11

Sunset, PA 13

July Fourth 15

City 16

Journey Home 17

Bow Down 18

Worth 23

Great Possessions 24

Eden 25

All the Buried Places 26

My Garden 30

Saving Bond 33

Indebted 36

Advent 41

Acts of Anxiety 49

Acts of Interpretation 50

Acts of Habit 52

Acts of Home 53

Acts of Fiction 54

Acts of Healing 56

Acts of Love 57

Acts of Vexation 58

Acts of Withdrawing 60

Acts of Will 61

Acts of Knowledge 62

Acts of Making 63

Do not save love
      for things
           Throw *things*
to the flood

Lorine Niedecker

Small Works

When Poverty Is Unattainable

When poverty is unattainable
as an aspiration

what use am I

a fanatical servant
to the sign

The country inside or
the "inner country"

discerns something

intends to translate the person
the animal body

For one seeks in vain
to be purged of excess

to be fortified
without a promise

What lodges or inheres
as identity

The random opening of the same
or similar passages

Portents or adequate frustration

for "becoming"
or seeming to remain

incorruptible

To each her own paradise

for nought but to keep
loneliness full of capacity

or furrowed with deceit

The marvel of "security"
breaks utterly as a saving remedy

Except what others give me
I am empty

a penitent, imitating less

Though I hunger and thirst

I am not an action figure
at your mercy

Behold
a wilderness of voices
crying within one

Pursuit

The tension created between proof
and devotion

When reveal becomes a lever
and you press it

your heart will feel gallantly
recreated

Forget Me Not

I walk from morning
into my ghost

a silent pulling
road to you

Is it memory or
wonder

we are reduced to
following

beyond promise

of recognition

A Charm for Sleep *for Nathaniel*

Fear has an ear
in it

and so it appears

on all sides of night

laden
with beasts

The hour "when"
The hour "until"

is the world's tribulation

To fall into history
To fall down a hole
To fall into the lion's jaws

So small
the ear appears

and yet, so laden
with the night's hours

The road to be taken
is most certainly

a rod
to be taken into one's own hands

A shepherd

you know the road, don't you

what the tiny foreleg holds

Your fear is an old snare

When concrete replaces nature

who can tell friend from foe

The road will appear laden

The whole world's tribulation

Your hearing, a surrogate belief

My fondness for a lamb

When I was small
I held on to a psalm

My balm was a lamb

Because night has a thing in it
that cannot be calmed

To lie down and weep
as the voice beckons

"Come and see"

Sleep is a charmed mystery

a dreaded runway

embedded with vanishings

To ward something off
draw it

and it will pass away

Discourse with it
and it will lose its magnitude

You will lay yourself down
uncaptured

Surely your soul will be kept
rescued in the sayings of this book

When rescue is secure
your reward is with you

And you are your own reward

Summer

My heart, this sunken day
I shall go on saying
Mercy
how the heat tires
determination
Upholds method
and prudence
in watering
And we all went out
to nightfall
And there was luxury in it

How to Stay Alive in the Woods

for Michael O'Leary

Mosquitoes prefer blue
and all birds are eatable

Suppose you have no gun
snares are simple and invaluable

A button is a useful lure
and the best belt has a buckle

Blood can be secured and carried
and bones may mean your salvation

Staying alive in the woods

from the green depths of sensation
From and into all the extensions of being "lost"

Perhaps it's not your road
where you reside

a crosswalk from one street to the next

Remember, anyone can build a lean-to
or start a fire without a match

Stretch out on the forest floor

Lie still
and without a path

Animals will come
very close

Sunset, PA

With just paper and pen

and begin a conversation

It is and how

crucial it is

that we do something special

Especially I could go there
during the winter

Alongside of descriptions

I have spent the details
to convince my skepticism

Altering our behavior at human presence

Your hundreds of excuses

Walk over to the fence

for the evidence
is in view

July Fourth

The plenty of this heat
annoys a family
in a habitat so concrete
Urges us to sleep
in spite of daylight
Down like dead leaves
migrants prefer darkness
When the sun consumes
the moon illumines
coasts and rivers
I have no quarrel
with winter

City

I've seen each day
distantly

Awoke to the sound
of cars parking

I've looked down littered alleys

The rivers on either side
of me

I've had enough
of this tenuous

intimacy

Take a look or ignore it

Always unsure

From which direction
the sun rose

Journey Home

The woods your shadow left

the color of green without rain

When we arrived

the sun kept us hidden

The chairs we wore in silence

Your house, a hill paved road

We held the baby way past dark

trying to listen

The foxes strained our eyes, to see

Everyone slept and rose early

Echoes of the soil I've not forgotten

how to run

Bow Down

The latch string pulled in

and it was *The End*

Sentiment

Coals covered over
Makes me eager to live closer

When my eyes can't remember

You can follow the color of autumn
the smell of rotted leaves
back to my heart

How it's made metaphoric

Held in place by a sharp stitch

Touch that is harmless and noiseless
is a rare reward

as unexpected as a death

With the snow and the trees
everything
appeared to be melting

At last
the mind wears out the best resolve
and cannot fast upon

what convictions rest in memory

Buttoning my coat to the last button

I never feel private

Faith comes to one noiseless
and yet, keeps one exasperated

Eager to touch touch

A bird's nest

How I pull my young
thread by thread out of my bed

Close my eyes

I am sewing a piece of cloth
across the cold

Where one's breath breaks

I have traced a heart
on the window glass

How odd it felt
How feelings can be an odd reward

To be touched by someone's eyes

The yearnings

the heart strings itself through
thread over thread

the saw-toothed edge of faith

Stitched into place

My flesh is clothed with

I have woven a nest of leaves

When I remember you

an unexpected memory
I am useless next to

Worth

Solomon's song
was longer than
a one night stand

Call it "devotional"
Love is ... the slow attainment
of disclosure

It fortifies the soul

It cleanses without displacing
more than it tenders

You have put off your coat
for less
and are bereft

for it is yet winter

O
thou wert as my brother
wrestling with my words
And I leaned my body into the sport
intent on proving my worth

Great Possessions

Three wooded acres

books or no books
I can walk over

Daybreak
from boundaries

This is my domain
Name

Eden

Endure has an end
you may rue
at the outset

But it also has need

and need is an Eden
(if you know what I mean)

Eden = Need

One and the same
the same

How I hold it

All the Buried Places *for Peter Gizzi*

All the buried places
will eventually find you

salvaged from a cold day

Everyone remembers
with a thread of hatred

So many years pulling after you
silent tethers of need

Something steps out from behind a tree
Merely an accumulation of leaves

Imagine it was your father coming back
so that you could pass through his membranes

hear his voice as it spoke

Whatever we lose
though we dream and hardly know it

will use us

so utterly itself and nothing else

You could speak to yourself
walking along a road

a movie running backwards
until it's dark

You could think you are speaking
and those inside would hardly know

what a cold day remembers
whistling under the window

Hatred and dearth
salvaged from a thread

You are pulled by
a familiar silence

Memory is not a fool

Everyone remembers
a thousand images of one gesture

The way a touch is tethered to you

and you wonder
how cold it is back East

Whatever you lose
will eventually find you

salvaging words from an accumulation of roads
where you are walking

My Garden

When the spirit is single

the body is a silver singing bird
a rounded water

"A garden enclosed is my sister"
completeness, harmony, and stillness

"A garden enclosed is my sister"
a moon lady surrounded by forest

"A garden enclosed is my sister"
standing on scissors and roses

My garden is enclosed in my sisters

Oh my sister, oh my spouse

if my love is too formidable
and forlorn

stay me with your laughter

and I shall not compare you
afterwards

Other to other as we are

I will carry you on my back

I will wash your feet and neck

because you are to me
life's vitality

A fountain to which
hands open
like Easter eggs

Nearness counts
twice that of the sun

Human or animal

When the body is single
the spirit is like a bird
in winter

Gone away or stayed
with nothing to feedeth upon

Asleep yet awakened
Awakened and yet not at home

Saving Bond *for Kate Josephson*

Say that the books
we sleep between

pressed our eyes into one image

Pulled from the binding

one sees oneself rushing to survive

We stand outside
We are waiting for the train

My heart is hardened against
My heart

Expectation is a crime
that has robbed me many a time

It is better to have nothing
To turn and have nothing

Lot's wife was salt and barren
Anonymous

She turned the page and was gone

Bound to the economy
I'm an incapacity

A worthless worth

An economic curse
upon the world

Who could buy a heart FOR SALE?

The cost of finding something
and then losing it

defies possession

No more nor less than

unfolding all to you

I sought to keep

Indebted

It was touching to see

To make the sky look smaller

Our shoes full of puddles

The strange secrets of color

In a charmed circle
two hours pretending to be ghosts

Seeking and being sought

Crows in the park

The last one home's a cocoon

Somebody's still sleeping
in my bed

Now we are humming

I love to hold onto something

Sew it to myself

The holes in my fingers
These patterns dress me

The strange charms of home

I love to hold a sleeping body

or pretend the smaller shoes my own

Roaming through morning

my face tightens to a crow's
call

Seeking to be sought

Your bed is now a boat

No need for food or drink

your head straight for the deep

When too long alone

I conjure a thunderstorm to bring you home

What you sought with your pirate eye
is but a ghost of our real hunger

I am taking you under my wing

Seeking charms I could never make out

you fill my shoes with stones

Now you're a ghost color

It was touching to see
the holes for your eyes

My face caught in a puddle
as wide as your arms

Seeking and being sought after

You sew the sky to your head

So only the moon can find you

Advent

Should you turn away your eyes
the mystery is mine
All subtlety and mischief
I will not be without
but swear I faith
and blow a kiss
only to be left groping
like, in the night, a thief
gropes after valuables
An unknown countenance
tensed in silence

The pestilence of pollution
is breath-taking
What is consumed
for the sake of living longer?
The flower fadeth
from the form
To be utterly undone
in an unknown tongue
Dear friend
we are in darkness
at home, within

No snow
but the cold blows us
so many days
away from the door
Nothing is more portentous
than the silence of neglecting
effort
Contaminated by state and statutory
appearance is usurped by authority
Toward the gallows tree of Hell
Secrets are ubiquitous

Are we nothing but beggars
seeking for joy
Some balm of mitigation
for the spirit's calm
recovery
before it becomes the eternity
it precedes
Alone
in a dove-like meekness
belied

When a memory is retained
what is recognized?
Should I turn away my eyes
you remain
the leaven hidden in the bread
I grope for
the door to your encounter
Giving me birth
to become a small child
My ardent desire
with such a companion

Without having any doubt
Feeling it
Movements like a game
At once our faces will change
to contain the invisible
When the phantasm is embraced
A double
A little aperture
The world as a picture
The locus where the rupture is
Through the window
an infinity of light

Acts

Acts of Anxiety

Ready or not
the day comes on

It sits upon us
with one accord

Anytime a door is opened
anywhere

Many are the expectations
amassed

And it shall come to pass

The world of consequence be with you
always

Acts of Interpretation

To become a kind of emissary
I have found
wonder
in pieces
moving towards me, slowly

All at once
the depths of time
abide
inside

A lantern on the internal
intensified

You can define prospect
with only so much

certainty

Rain pooled in the streets' hollows

I swallow the news

Someone is gambling
for control

If you don't mind
just sitting there
to be moved

Acts of Habit

Tear it apart
and it comes back again

A spider's web rebuilt at dawn

With nothing wasted
Does not change with the times

So earthly and ancient

The myth of morning
The morning makes us

Acts of Home

Earned is to endeavor

as the already familiar ones
surround me

A cosmos of hands lending a hand

Subsequently
a substantial part of
my real substance

Knock knock
I'm here
till the cows come

Home

Acts of Fiction

The legend of
      the beginning of the world
speaks thus:
      We had climbed all the steps
when a most beautiful Dog smiled.

I took courage and asked,
"Who are you?"

The Dog Tongue said:
"I belong to the body. Both
in summer and winter
I am hungry for what is hidden
in the heart."

I turned. I saw a door open
between my confessions.
On it were written these words:

    The animals are angels

I then drew near the earth with
bended knee. The flowers were
so small and bright.
The birds were glowing like stars.

Acts of Healing

That you healed when you were ill

Not grateful then
you lived

to yourself alone

Speechless
a stranglehold

found gripping
the mind and immortal soul

What is bound within?

You go on
washing your face, hands

All of the parts

Acts of Love

If endear is earned
and is meant to identify
two halves

then it composes
one meaning

which means
a token

a knot
a note

a noting in the head
of how it feels

to have your heart
be the dear one

Acts of Vexation

The only thing under the sun
I can run to
is Ecclesiastes

for there is nothing gathered into one self
that can be kept

Want is humbled by death
as every purpose manifests it

Feeling this all my life
a piercing fright
gathers in the stomach's pit

This is it and this is not the end
of the road

for even despair is a kind of goad
to wisdom

The beauty of the world
over one's own anguish

The day that I lost all feeling

I was both a Fool and a Goddess

Acts of Withdrawing

As in every hour
of unquenchable passion
or starving faith

I hold out

knowing nothing
but the quiet
of chaotic concentration

An anxious discipline
bestowed upon the mind's
gradual restoration to function

Solace bridles life's logical desperation

A paradise of loneliness

incurred

Acts of Will

Let me open up
like morning down my spine

and find that I have found

no clear route
no evident map of destination

only a constant disappearing
into the day's allowance

Acts of Knowledge

As if a book
were a kind of
voluntary nurse

looking for the wound
inside you

Words and senses
Terror and delicacy

Wisdom

The leaves on the tree
grew

Acts of Making

Small intensities
work into the nervepulse

relentlessly dislocating significance

A makeshift wildness

the hand transcribes
and joins

Born in New Cumberland, Pennsylvania, **Pam Rehm** currently lives in New York City with her husband and two children. She is the author of five previous collections including *Gone to Earth* (Flood Editions, 2001). From 1994–97, she was an editor of the poetry journal *apex of the M*.